INTERIOR FITNESS

Move Your Heart

To Reshape Your Life
AND Your Body!

DIOFITNESS, INC.

By:

Migdoel Miranda
World-Class Trainer, Speaker and Authority On
The Mind-Body Training Connection

DIOFITNESS, INC.

Published by
DioFitness, Inc.
Austin, TX

www.DioFitness.com

This book is dedicated to my believers, especially to:

Kai, my 5-year old son - for keeping me creative, passionate, and loving. Your smile touches my heart. Your life is so pure! I enjoy your existence.

Kamila, my 2-year old daughter – for your unique presence – even without words, we feel your thoughts and desires. Thank you for crying and fighting for what you really want. That always moves me to want to let you win!

Nicole, my wife - for trusting me and for your calm demeanor that balances me, so that I can think!

My parents and siblings - for letting me fly from a very young age, for releasing me and letting me be myself, for doubting me & my unique ideas, which propelled me forward even farther.

My good friends - for listening to my personal life story and respecting my heart.

Foreword

As soon as I became a dad, I began to question if there were other ways of achieving optimal fitness. I had been trained, educated, and practiced in conventional fitness techniques throughout my time as a professional baseball player and after my subsequent certification as a high-level fitness trainer. Just having the thought that there might be an alternative way of training went against everything I had ever learned and represented up until that moment.

As I watch my two children innocently at play, it makes me aware that true physical freedom, vitality, and fitness are not about the classic mile markers of weights, measuring body fat, increasing/decreasing intensity, tempos, repetitions, or sets. While I realized this goes against my entire formal college education and experience, and the entire classic fitness industry model, I realized that authentic physical fitness is actually all about free movements in the natural world and is a product of one's interior state of mind. Real strength is not predicated upon the limited 'no pain, no gain' approach, but rather about feeling a sense of health and vitality from within.

One of the revolutionary illuminations that I had is that fitness can simply be waking up in the morning with no pain. Fitness is having your emotions aligned with your spirit. This inner alignment is reflected outwardly via your physical posture and breathing. When you are fit on the inside, you do not reject those who use their life to teach lessons of love, but rather embrace the abstract emotions as powerful life forces. To be physically fit means to be present with yourself in every moment without blaming others for what has happened in your life. Whatever has happened to you thus far in your life is a result of your own prior decision-making. Your comfort level with this will determine how fit you are. Determining how fit you are from day to day can only be achieved by taking time to be with yourself. That level of fitness is an attitudinal barometer of your own abilities and gratitude towards everything in your life.

I wanted to write this book because throughout the fitness industry there is unnecessary pain associated with workouts. This pain is counterproductive and not essential for helping you reach your fitness goals. In fact, this pain often takes the form of emotional pain resulting from bullying by coaches or personal trainers, which ultimately sabotages your interior fitness, and therefore, lessens your overall physical fitness. Many clients often suffer intense personal shame as a result of this training technique. The client walks away from a training session and feels a complete lack of appreciation for who they are and the talents they demonstrated. In order to cope with this negative coaching energy, clients frequently disassociate from themselves and their interior fitness so that they can alleviate this sense of failure that is being externally imposed upon them by these Hitleresque pseudo coaches. A workout filled with negativity and emotional pain will never get you to your desired level of exterior or interior fitness.

The purpose of this book is to raise your awareness of the power of your mind, the power of forgiveness, the power of self-love, and to show you that the path to true fitness is to get physically fit outside the gym in natural environments.

I am not against gym environments per se, because they have been a big part of my life and success as an athlete. However, I am much more supportive of doing the inner work that makes the outer results a lot easier to achieve, whether you are a professional athlete or just want to feel good. There are times when lifting weights and traditional training techniques can be beneficial.

Lifting heavy things is cool and reveals part of you, but lifting yourself from the inside out demonstrates a much greater capacity for true fitness. It is what I call the path of 'interior fitness'. What resides in your interior is what is reflected in your exterior. Your interior fitness is the secret ingredient to having the inner edge on living your life to your peak performance daily.

This book is best read with an open mind. If you continue to think the same thoughts you have always had, you will continue to get the same results. By expanding your perspective and learning a new way of thinking, you can change your fitness results. Embrace the innocent sensation of a beginner's mind in order to allow these new ideas to penetrate into your workout experience.

The best thing about this book is that it gives me the chance to show others how I have made myself a better person by incorporating these concepts into my own daily life. Allow yourself to likewise be inspired to move your heart in new ways, which will reshape your life and your body. Then, share these new concepts with the people you love, so that they can reshape their lives and their bodies to be and feel their best too.

To Your Interior Fitness

Migdoel "Dio" Miranda
Celebrity Trainer & Founder, DioFitness, Inc.

Table of Contents

Chapter One: Get Out Of the Gym

"If you think you are too small to make a difference,
try sleeping with a mosquito in the same room."
~ The Dalai Lama

My approach to coaching is to meet people at their level. To literally set myself aside for a little while and welcome their life, so that I can better help them. By building a bridge of authentic connection through compassion and seeing life through their eyes, I understand their world better and can help them understand how fitness, both interior and exterior, can have a tremendously positive impact on their entire well-being.

Having worked for more than a decade with a range of people at various fitness levels, from professional athletes to amateur competitors, to men and women reclaiming their health and maintaining good fitness, I have seen all the avoidance tricks that people use to get out of going to the gym, including:
- Being too busy to workout.
- Not finding time to eat or prepare good food.
- Working too many hours at a job.
- Caving into a sabotaging partner or family member.
- Making their workout routine too demanding to the point they no longer want to participate because it no longer brings them joy.
- Making negative comparisons of their weight, fitness, self-esteem to others.

This is all totally normal.

One of the things I find most ironic about fitness is that it is actually the lack of fitness that keeps us from enjoying certain opportunities in life. And yet, when life calls us forward and we participate, we are naturally fit. As just one example, many people choose to not go into the military because they do not like rules, restrictions, and discipline. But if they did go into the military, they would be physically active, and the discipline inherent in that structure, in that environment, would help their body get more fit and feel better, and get paid for it! Rather than letting the fear of what it takes to be fit stop us, jump into life! Get out of the gym and be fit by living your life naturally!

By responding to your body's normal, natural tendencies toward movement, and consuming healthy food to meet your physical needs, you change the chemistry of your brain and other body systems. You release natural happy hormones called endorphins that bring a sense of joy, which positively reinforces your exercise routine and makes you want to do it again. It is fun! Your skin glows. People are attracted to you because it is obvious that you take care of yourself and feel good. You become naturally magnetic when you listen to your body's natural rhythms for self-care. When you try different exercise routine options and you have these results, then you know that you have found a great fitness routine for yourself.

One of the most common misconceptions my new clients have about fitness is that you have to be tough to be fit. The reality is that as you increase your fitness levels, you build your resilience and endurance. You become stronger as you become more fit. In fact, many times you will be stronger than your typical trainer because your trainer is not as motivated to do for themselves what you are doing for yourself with their help.

One of the most important things you can do is to find a trainer or coach who actually believes in you and your possibilities, rather than imposing his ways upon you. If you find someone who is not at least as high on life in their attitude, outcomes, and goals as you are, then you would be doing yourself a disservice to hire that individual. I know this to be true because when I practiced only traditional strength training, I used to eat Snickers in between client sessions! I was preaching and teaching one thing, and living another. Once I decided to 'own' my personal integrity, all that changed. My intention is to be completely transparent, so that you can see that even world-class trainers are human and had to start where you may find yourself now. That is, with imperfections in their fitness routines and life practices.

While many go-getters and type-A personalities will push while in training just to survive a grueling workout, they do not finish with a sense of increased vitality and well-being. They are merely beating themselves up. In the long run, many of these people suffer from adrenal fatigue. Functionally, this is the lost ability to deal with stressful situations at the hormonal level. The consequence is to feel tired all the time. They may be energetic, but exhausted underneath. They may suffer from respiratory infections, allergies, asthma, chronic fatigue syndrome, frequent colds, hypoglycemia and addictions, such as alcoholism, amongst other conditions. The resulting behaviors might be judged by others as being lazy and/or unmotivated, but these behaviors are a result of a physical condition that causes mental sluggishness and physical lack of initiative.

If the medical community would pay attention to adrenal fatigue, there would be no need for medication in many cases, because this causal condition of so many diseases would be dealt with from the beginning. When you are connected to yourself, your body will send signals in the form of symptoms in order to get your attention so you can do something about what is destabilizing you and you can respond by making necessary adjustments. Through my experience, I have discovered that the best interior and exterior fitness can be found in the basics, rather than the fancy extensive scientific labs and high-end training facilities. There is a time and place for everything and, I believe, the place to begin is strengthening your interior fitness. To learn more about adrenal fatigue yourself, an excellent resource is: Adrenal Fatigue: The 21st Century Stress Syndrome by James L. Wilson, N.D., D.C., PhD. and Jonathan V. Wright, M.D.

In my philosophy, the 'no pain, no gain' mentality that is pervasive in the traditional training world, has done more to 'kill' than heal human bodies. It doesn't help anyone to experience physical pain caused by a workout. Soreness and pain are characteristic of broken muscle tissue and metabolic waste. The 'no pain, no gain' mentality is very old school and many times an assassin of positive fitness. You cannot hurt your way to health or fitness.

Instead, you need to find your personal 'zone' during your fitness training to both enjoy and benefit from it. That is why a good trainer will assess rather than make assumptions about your conditioning, preferences, and lifestyle choices. If you do not enjoy your fitness sessions, you will not want to follow through with them because they will feel more like punishment than a pathway to health and fitness. However, if you orient your heart and mind properly in addition to your workout routine, then you will naturally move your body through your life in a new way and become physically fit more naturally.

The grass is greener now and is waiting for you. You do not need to experience the revolving doors of a dark, dusty gym in order to feel good. Breathing dirty air, comparing yourself to others in the mirrors, and dealing with trainers who can sell you a car as well as a 36-session package in the name of commitment, is disrespectful to your body, and shows lack of integrity towards this beautiful profession called 'personal training and coaching.'

Besides, oftentimes it is the "wannabe" models and bodybuilders who are most active in such gyms and they are not the epitome of good health, but rather excess. Beware of the superficial appeal of this type of fitness.

True fitness is not merely exterior superficiality, but rather has to include interior fitness as well.

Fitness is not solely about looking good, having muscles, or how clear your skin is, but in addition, fitness should be defined via the more intangible concepts of wellness, peacefulness, loving, and practicing forgiveness. Fitness also shows through daily physical body functions. For example, barring social norms, you could ask any body builder, fitness model, or even the average Joe who drains himself or herself in the gym daily, about their physical elimination habits (as in, do you poop daily) and, unfortunately, you would find many times that the answer would be no. To be healthy, you should poop not only daily, but copiously, a great amount of elimination is an indicator that you are eating properly and everything is flowing through your system. In fact, 12 inches in length is ideal for a single elimination in the average size person. Being fit has both inner and outer expressions. To learn more on healthy elimination practices, read the book How to Eat, Move and Be Healthy by Paul Chek, HHP.

The kind of work that leads to true fitness has nothing to do with counting calories or with weighing your food. It has to do with the feeling that you get while moving forward or backwards with your life, depending on which way your fitness is heading. For instance, by restricting resentment and gossip, you may lose unwanted weight faster than calorie counting and going to the gym because your interior changes your exterior. Even your motivation for getting fit will make a difference. For example, are you doing the work to get fit because of your own desires or because someone else wants you to get fit? Obviously, you will have greater success when your own desire for fitness is your motivating factor. Fitness is achieved through self-love, not pleasing someone else.

We are spiritual beings having a human experience. Being human means taking care of your physical body, which includes the main contributors of good health: nutrition and exercise. Your body expresses various symptoms to communicate to you an imbalance, including the energetic or spiritual level. That is a call for your loving response towards your body to take care of it. For example, when we try to trap our spirit and limit our freedom by staying stuck in unhealthy relationships or habits, our body will oftentimes rebel by gaining weight or even feeling physical pain.

Your spirit desires freedom and communion with nature. Your backyard, the park, and the beach can be your best gym. They are free, with fresh, clean air and feel-good vibes. These places in nature welcome you as you are without the false pretense of mirrors or someone spinning by your side. You do not need the artificial mirrors of the gym or someone to compete with. The only thing needed is your presence. The moment is yours. Your heart at work is as natural as the rhythm of the rain. Your sincerity is your natural armor. Your inner spirit has room to dance without an audience. It is in this amazingly peaceful place where you should experience your uniquely beautiful essence, and really commune with who you are at your core.

How you work on yourself makes the greatest difference. If you do not enjoy the fitness exercise that you are participating in, you will not want to do it. It is like interviewing for your dream job, running a marathon, or passing a life-changing exam when nobody else is looking. You are improving yourself for you, not someone else's approval. This is about you being the best you can be, not the best that others can be or expect from you. Comparison to others has no place in your interior or exterior fitness program. This is when you honor your Creator by being a good steward of the physical body you've been given for this lifetime.

Having worked in and around professional sports for many years, I know what happens behind the scenes with people whom the public has placed on a pedestal. Through quiet personal observation, I have seen that being a celebrity is not the glamorous experience that is portrayed in media hype and reporting; in fact, many of these celebrities would rather trade lives with you. Their lives are not what you might think, so once again, comparison serves nobody and is only a fantasy. Craving anyone else's life experience is like putting diesel gas in a car that requires unleaded fuel: it just will not work right. Your only job is to be your best self.

If you do want to be a celebrity in your own life, go out and live it all the way by being healthy, happy, real, and whole. Videotape your successes and share them via YouTube to inspire others to do the same. These days, everyone takes their phone with them, so make your life so happy, full, and real that even your own cell phone wants to follow you!

As a trainer, one of the keys to my professional success has been assessing the entirety of my clients. My intention is to help my clients care for their fitness holistically so that I can better assess what issues, besides physical fitness, might arise during the course of our journey together.

One of the first things I do with my clients is to teach them to empty what the Buddhists call the 'monkey mind.' Monkey mind is a term that describes the racing thoughts and mental churn that most of us have as we try to get through our complex daily lives with too much to do. Of course, this requires me to empty my own mind, turn off my phone, and be completely available to those who invest in their own healing process through fitness.

Once we have achieved a clear mental space to begin training, I assess my client's fitness from four different vantage points: physical, emotional, mental, and spiritual. Many times my clients seek support for a physical limitation, but in reality, this is only an outer manifestation of underlying internal constriction revealing itself. In some cases, additional expertise is required to remove the emotional, mental, or spiritual blockage in order for my clients to progress to a higher level of both physical and inner fitness. In such cases, I'm happy to recommend a professional in other disciplines who will help ensure success in my clients' fitness quest.

My initial assessment is based on my professional observations, the client's preliminary written self-assessments, a dialogue of questions and answers and, finally, an evaluation of bio motor skills. The bio motor skills assessment considers a client's current conditioning in terms of strength, endurance, power, flexibility, agility, coordination and balance as well as various other measurements, such as spinal, degree of flexibility, etc.

The types of movements that reveal a person's primal skills assessment include: squats, lunges, twisting, pushing, pulling, walking, running, jogging and bending. These are considered core functional movements and therefore are the keys to physical fitness. This is also how we determine a baseline condition in order to assess future fitness progress.

Once we understand the baseline condition, I create a personalized plan that is appropriate for that person's lifestyle and baseline condition to help them achieve their fitness goals. The magical elements that really make this plan work are easy to do because they are enjoyable, it feels good and naturally integrates into the client's lifestyle, creating a customized plan for them that also works in a natural setting such as the backyard, park, or beach.

This is one of my primary goals, as these are environments where interior fitness can flourish. It is quintessential to get out of the gym to feel good, create vital health, and experience positive fitness.

Take a Moment For Your Interior Fitness:

- Take a few minutes each day to contemplate your life and appreciate it.
- Go out and look at the stars so as to feel your place in the cosmic plan with a fresh perspective.
- Leave the gym and spend at least thirty minutes being active outside in nature, take deep breaths, use expansive 'stretch' movements, and challenge your major muscle groups with squats, push-ups and sit-ups.

Get Out of the Gym- People do not need more weights or to be surrounded by people in order to connect with themselves. When people workout, they are really looking to connect with themselves, initially physically, but hopefully eventually, more emotionally. Working out is a form of meditation. Meditation is an inside journey that does not focus on the outside, but its positive effects are reflected on the outside.

Chapter Two: Let Go For Lift-off

"If you are brave enough to say goodbye,
life will reward you with a new hello."
~ Paulo Coelho

As a punishment for misconduct, pilots sometimes get grounded. The same thing happens to you when your heart is anchored in what does not serve you. This misconduct is oftentimes self-inflicted and includes anything that feels bad, takes away your power, keeps you small, or marginalizes your contribution. These toxic effects can take on many forms of expression in your life such as a relationship, an entrenched habit, bad career choice, a bad behavior, or negative self-talk. Whatever form the self-misconduct takes, you must let go of it in order stop being grounded and to have lift-off in your life.

Ironically, your 'enemies' are your greatest teachers. You do not want to order their assassination; rather, you want them to find peace. They are present in your life to help you grow to a higher spiritual level. The people or situations that you per-ceive as enemies are present in your life to cause trouble, cause pain, or otherwise get our attention because they serve you by revealing to you those parts of yourself that even you do not want to face. These are the ugly parts of us as human beings that we try to avoid because they present themselves in hateful, painful ways. This causes cortisol and adrenaline to jack-up our bodies for a while, stress us out physically and psychologically, and take a toll on those around us with our over-amped behavior. Being pumped full of these two hormones can make you feel like the world is your enemy, and you may end up fighting with the ones who love you as a defense mechanism for survival. This ugly side is like a shadow that comes to teach us new life lessons. Enemies teach us more positive, productive ways of dealing with adversity that will bring us to a place of peace instead of conflict. These innovative thoughts will help to wipe away our pain and suffering and raise us up. For instance, when we are sad, feeling out of control, feeling powerless, or when our anger turns inward, those are the shadowy parts of our being that come to teach us and ultimately prepare us for lift-off.

When you find out that another person is merely the messenger of a lesson and not an enemy, then you realize that the key is forgiveness and not hatred. Forget retaliation. Instead, search inside yourself for peace! Allow your brain to be still and obedient to your heart. It is time to follow your heart and in some magically surprising ways, always be guided safely to shore.

Sometimes it is only blind faith that will get you through a difficult situation. If you find yourself in a body you do not recognize, a life that does not make you happy, or a relationship that feels toxic, all it means is that you did not know something at the time you made the decisions in your past that you know now. It is all designed to help you get to a higher level in the greatest sense. When you have this revelation, you might think that the Almighty One is not on your side, know that He is, just in a different way than you thought. Once you have this revelation, you have the responsibility to evolve spiritually and move forward to a greater level of interior fitness. Your life matters! Your best life is waiting for you in every moment. It is up to you to look within and move forward.

"So I prayed, but I had to pray from my heart. All of my concentration and thoughts went from my head to my heart. All of my senses - hearing, smell, taste, and feeling - were connected to my heart."
~ Wallace Black Elk

One of the times I had to divinely trust beyond what I could see was both one of the lowest and highest times of my life. I had graduated from college in Tennessee, moved to Atlanta, which did not suit me, and was on my second post-college destination of Dania, Florida. I had rented a room in a friend's mom's house and quickly got a serving job within walking distance but knew I needed something better. I needed to broaden my horizons. I asked to borrow my friend's mother's bike and rode it daily for an entire year and took a job farther away at a different restaurant. I biked because I did not have the money to take the bus to my new job at Tony Roma's in Hallandale. Why did I choose this particular restaurant? I chose it because it was located next to Premier Health and Fitness. My gut was telling me that in order to get to my next level of interior fitness I needed to get back to the world I loved of personal training. I innately knew that Premier Health and Fitness was going to be the key to that.

During the second year of my work, I was earning enough money to take the bus to my job and the gym. During my bus journeys, I enjoyed conversations that I would never hear otherwise, about important things like the need to get to a destination for a job or to pick up food. I learned that the driver would not speak unless I started the conversation, but once it was started, it was evident that he actually craved that personal connection.

My destiny at the gym began with a job of re-racking the weights and sweeping the floors. While this may seem beneath a college-educated athlete, it actually opened the door for me to gain a deeper knowledge of my trade of personal training. Here I met a beautiful soul named Adita Yrizarry. She was in charge of all the classes and personal training. I tried hard from day one to impress upon her my desire to be a trainer at the gym, not only a trainer, but the best trainer, and quickly. This very special person was sent by God to show me things about myself that even I did not know but needed to be revealed to me. She believed in me, nourished me, and taught me in my most desperate moments how to value myself. With dignity, peace, pain, and sweat, I gathered myself to rise up and seize this opportunity. I stood straight, reduced the size of my ego, respected myself in new ways, and off I went to start the journey to become me, the person that I am today.

So, the days went by, and I was earning money by waiting tables at Tony Roma's, but the paycheck was not enough to cover all my meager living expenses. Many times, I survived by eating soup and lots of bread in between waiting tables because I was hungry. I also began taking with me 'clean' leftovers from my tables as food to eat when I got home. I recall the sweat running hard and fast down my chest when I did take those leftovers because, while there were no specific rules about taking food that would have been thrown away anyway, I felt like I was risking my job. Yet, despite this risk, I did it again and again, day after day, as I needed it to feed myself. I never told anyone.

Nobody knew my inner pain. I had some close friends at the time that I now realize God placed in my life so that I was not so lonely. He had them watching over me as his Angels without my knowing it at the time. They were part of something magical, like Adita. There were days I was so tired that my legs carried me to where I had to go daily without my even noticing the streets. Those were the days that I think my team of Angels were carrying me and pedaling that bike, as I was far too exhausted to do it by myself under my own power. The Angels carried me for quite a while. They placed me on my bed at night and woke me early in the morning. I was living as close to divinity as I ever had. It was full of simplicity. I was never late for work and always had enough energy to fulfill my duties there. It was like living a dream within a dream. I was present physically, but being run by God's fuel. I just did not have any fuel of my own. I was eating poorly, working long hours, toiling at menial tasks. I felt that I was having an out of body experience. I rode that bike in the dark most days which was very scary, but I rarely feared because I had Angels as enforcers around me throughout my daily journey. Even though I am a pretty solid guy, somehow I felt light on that bike. All I had was my dream of becoming the best trainer and coach that I could be and God was conspiring to make it come true.

When I graduated from biking to taking the bus, I walked by what is today the Diplomat Hotel in Hallandale, FL. I was humbled by my sweaty trek through the mud of what was, in those days, the hotel's construction site. Much like me, the hotel was under construction. Instead of feeling anger as I dredged through mud, I felt connected to it as our construction and reconstruction processes melted together. Anytime I feel mud and sweat now, it reminds me of my own growth.

When someone suffers that long and at that level, something is sure to crack. For me, that day came when I screamed at God so loudly that I think He heard me at the physical level. While I had been taught that the way to converse with God was through silent prayer, I could not stop screaming at the top of my lungs because I wanted to provoke Him to pay attention to my suffering and me. I was feeling a level of pain and fear that penetrated through every cell of my physical body and screaming was the only way I knew how to communicate that. It cleared the doubts in my head, gave clarity to my life, and reminded me of where I belonged. I felt compelled to shout my rage and pain and that it was ENOUGH already. I was giving everything I had to make a solid go at life, had sacrificed so much, and it was time for a change. I needed a movement forward and was determined to shout my way there if necessary.

One week later, I owned a car. I could finally stop meeting friends at the bus stop. I could sleep a little more and allow my brain and body to rest. It was the pivotal point that turned around my life where I pictured God laughing because my desperation was merely a single step towards my main goal in life of getting back to fitness. Seeing Him laugh was a powerful picture that brought an odd sense of tranquility to me. I became aware that I had been in powerful company all the time, even when I was covering my ears. My heart kept following the clear, but blind, advice to never give up. It was when I screamed and imagined him laughing as a benevolent Father, that I knew I had reached a turning point in my life. I cried! My own tears soothed my pain. I finally understood what having faith truly meant.

Maybe you are at a turning point like mine and it is what caused you to pick up this book. I know that everyone reaches these pivotal points in life. It is not a matter of whether they will happen, but rather when they will happen, and what you choose to do about them makes the difference.

One of the ways I describe the difference between the agony of fighting and the peace that comes with cooperation to my clients is to use my own experiences to show the contrast between then and now. It is the difference between the red waters created by the carnage left by those who fight the physical and mental fights to accomplish their dreams and the clear blue waters that are smooth and easy to navigate in simple elegance. When you do what you can and surrender the rest to your higher power, claim what is rightfully yours and honor the truth of you came to this Earth to be, then you will sail in the clear blue waters of an open sea.

In other words, you must release what does not work in your life in order for your life to take off in new ways. This means habits, relationships, routines, attitudes, mindsets, and language. The interior path to fitness is even more rigorous than the physical one, but it produces far superior results in the long run when you are willing to: 1) Honor who you are at your core, 2) Have integrity between what you say and what you do, 3) Feel the alignment between your inner and outer world on every level, 4) Honor your fitness as the piece of paper honors the tree, as an essential outcome of sacred structure.

Let go to lift-off. Keep your honor and life will always reward you.

Take a Moment For Your Interior Fitness:
- Do not weigh yourself for 30 days so you avoid setting yourself up for potential disappointment as your weight can fluctuate greatly during your initial program.
- Nourish your metabolism by eating every 2 to 4 hours.
- Evaluate your habits, routines, self-talk, relationships, leisure activities, perceptions, career, as well as how you spend your time / energy / resources to eliminate practices that feel incongruent with what you desire to experience. Find them and then take action to change them, one at a time.
- Be silent and pray daily and deeply. Let your heart flow in surrender and grace. Breathe through your heart. Ask for insight and support from your higher power. Feel the serenity that comes from knowing that you are loved in the greatest sense.
- Go stand in blue water, or dangle your feet on the edge of a pool. Allow yourself to smile with pleasure, to activate your good hormones and feel good all over.

Let Go For Lift-Off- Let go of negative feelings of disempowerment. To lift-off, you must wake up and recognize that what you need to succeed, you already have. As we pass through negative experiences in our lives, try not to hold on to the sadness of the lesson learned, just the lesson. Experience the emotion, and then leave it in the past. Encourage yourself to do positive activities that empower you.

Chapter Three: Self-Talk Without a Net

"It is not hard to make decisions once you know what your values are." ~ **Roy E. Disney**

You know what you value when you look around you right now at your life. What is most important to you? The clues to your values are in the books on your shelves, the people in pictures displayed in your home, the way in which you arrange your possessions in your space. These are small clues as to what you feel is important to you in your life.

Most people go through their life unconsciously, without thought of what they value most, and then they wonder why they are not as happy as they could be, why they have committed to too many things, or why they seem stuck in an occupation, relationship, or an environment they know they do not want.

Your values are the personal truths that you stand on to live your life. If you do not know them, you are at the mercy of your needs, which could lead to selfish and often negative or counter-productive behaviors. Once you discover and clarify your value system, it will serve as a framework for making future decisions.

Becoming clear about your personal life values serves your fitness because you will increase your power to choose how to live your life. Your values act as a powerful choice filter and magnet, attracting people and opportunities that enrich and serve your life. Life becomes easier and much more fulfilling as you live consciously.

The process of identifying your values is as simple as asking, 'What is most important for me in my life?' Dig deep by going past what comes up easy. Ask again. If you have a hard time deciding, let it go for a while and keep the question in the back of your mind. You will start to notice what you value. As they come up, add them to the list. Then start making choices based on your personal values. And know that any obstacles that show up are just a test to your commitment to living in congruence with your values. When you stand true to yourself, you will enjoy your rewards.

Now this all sounds really wise, but it took me years to figure it out! I began to have crucial conversations with myself when I realized that I had to get real traction if I wanted to edge toward my goals and dreams.

What I did not know is that you have to be ready to be knocked to the ground occasionally along the way. And when this happens, it really hurts! But hitting the hard floor does have a bright spot it reminds that you cannot go down any further even if you wanted to. The universal law of gravity may keep you physically grounded, but the universal law of growth says that you should go upward growing taller, bigger, with your head held high.

For me, the seed to my growth was found in really connecting deeply with the happy moments of my childhood. I had to get beyond living for mere survival and chasing money. I had to have honest conversations with myself to call out my self-truths. I had to do it without a mirror because I did not want any distortions to give me a reason to be distracted. I had to really meet myself without a net to save me from what I might find in my own stories. That was when I learned the importance of closing my eyes and acknowledging Whose powerful and unique presence I was entering.

Here's what I told myself:

"You do not know everything - embrace that. In fact, you do not know anything! The more you learn, the more you will find out that you do not know much. You do not know what you do not know and you probably do not know what you think you know. Be ok with it. Open your mind so you can really live. Be ok with your own mysteries!"

These simple words gave me permission to go beyond where I'd been to new places of insight. I gained new freedom in understanding myself. I learned that some of the stories I told about myself and others, to others and myself, were really just lies. I knew they were lies because of how I felt: hatred towards myself and others, discomfort, confusion, and a sense that 'God had done this to me' on purpose. Lies do not feel good. If an internal story makes you feel small, bad, or like a victim, it is a lie, no matter who implanted it in your mind!

The stories you tell yourself are little mini programs like the ones you would install on your computer. The more stories you tell yourself, the more entrenched your stories get over time. And then, to add insult to injury, we often have the need to convince other people to think like we do in order to validate ourselves. We do it for a sense of belonging to a tribe, and for many other reasons. The lies make sense to us in that moment but, really, are just our unmet needs projected out into the world. It is our job to go inside ourselves and understand why we think the way we do, and why we are so interested in convincing others to think the same way.

"People lie to you because you expect perfection and because we are not perfect and, well, there you go!"
~ Migdoel Miranda

My 5-year old son, Kai, has taught me to see life in a new way. He loves dinosaurs, but of course, he's never seen one alive. None of us has, and yet we have stories about the sequence of the dinosaurs' lives. We have created stories of how we think they must have once lived. The same is applied to the stories you tell yourself. Your stories can get in the way of doing what you know you can do to create the results you want to create!

Do you notice every time you talk to an elderly person they see you as so young? It is because we are always young! Stop those stories that say anything different and own the real you, the one that is young at heart. Do not look in the mirror, do not weigh yourself, and stop the body fat testing. These all rely on something external to give lifeless answers. The results depend on the tester, the quality of the mirror, and what you think the results should be.

On the one hand, stories help us to organize and share information to create bonds with other people. Stories can be wonderful and revered teaching tools which get passed down through generations, much like parables and fairy tales. Stories paint word pictures to help give voice to our visions.

And then there are stories that act as defense mechanisms, which signal a distress pattern or become a rationalization for doing something that is not right. How many of the following stories do you recognize for yourself?

- I cannot do 'that' yet because I am not ready / do not have the resources / did not do something else that has to be done first.

- I cannot focus on my fitness because I do not know what to do or how to fit it into my already full schedule.

- I want to hire a trainer and eat better but I do not have the money. I hear many people say this after buying the latest iPhone!

- I want to take time for my fitness but it means taking time away from my children or family.

- I wish I could do more for my health but I do not have enough time / money / training / etc.

If even one of these excuses hits home on any level with you, your story could be 'hooking' you and causing a limitation or rationalization that is making bad decisions for you. It is literally taking your power because you are subconsciously giving it away. Find the hidden motive within so you can consciously change it.

Knowing what your story is takes courage and is the first step in creating new, and often dramatic results. For the benefit of your interior fitness, you have to strip away the stories and imprinted patterns, even the ones that could be coming from other people, or other sources outside of you, so that you can get to the heart of what is your own true reality.

I grew up smoking as a child, even though I have never in my life smoked a cigarette. I was constantly exposed to second-hand smoke. I grew up physically fighting, yet I do not fight. From these experiences, I learned what it is like to push back from the things you know as 'normal' in order to break through to be true to yourself. As my good mentor once taught me, "get a backbone." Live what you believe to be true. Stop the stories you tell yourself that keep you stuck, small, or unhealthy so that you can achieve your optimal fitness faster and easier.

In fact, stories that are told about someone else that are not true or blown out of proportion are considered gossip. Caroline Myss, spiritual teacher and author, says, *"Stop gossiping. It is lethal and is affecting your cell tissue. It is that serious."* That is definitely also true for the negative stories you tell about yourself, both inside your own head and to other people. Do not let your past dictate your future fitness.

Change really only takes an instant. Stop now and smile, be thankful for breathing, as the single act of breathing is life at its best. By focusing on cleaning up your mindset, noticing your own self-talk or self-stories, you are noticing your own values and creating a rich foundation for new fitness levels.

For the inner journey of fitness to be done well, you must go deep and give up your current routines. This might upset the people in your support circles. By confronting the darkest parts of yourself, coming to grips with your gremlins, and dancing with your shadow, you are potentially looking for adversity. The goal is to be whole in the end.

People talk about 'as one door closes another opens', but nobody really talks about the long hallways in the middle. Those corridors can test even those who appear the strongest from the outside. By feeling the fear of what you might find within, working with your mindset and staying in action, you are taking the most significant hero's journey you could possibly undertake. But it is also one of the sources of true fitness. To thy own self be true. This includes all parts of you.

Talking to yourself without a net can feel like you are jumping out of an airplane, which can be a really scary feeling at the beginning, but eventually, you relax and just enjoy the ride and believe you can fly. And so you do! The belief that you can fly is the critical change of your mindset because you can no longer see the world as you did before. Now everything is possible.

Take a Moment For Your Interior Fitness:
- Today, for one day, do nothing - REST HARD!
- Tomorrow morning, smile when you get up and carry that smile to your mirror.
- If you are disturbed by anything outside your control such as a construction detour, your neighbors' dog barking, or a delayed flight, try to reframe and be in gratitude for what you do have. You have the ability to take a new route, to pray or meditate, to have more time to make a call or sing your favorite song in the privacy of your own car.
- Talk to yourself in the mirror! Look at your face and ask yourself who is looking at it and you will see how your perception changes.
- Be humble. You are the embodiment of one tiny bunch of cells in the huge orchestration of time and space. By recognizing that you are here to grow and do not know everything, you create room for new experiences and, more importantly, relationships.

Self-Talk Without A Net- Be honest when expressing yourself. Set achievable goals. Make promises to yourself. Do not be too harsh, just be honest. You have everything that you need right now to move forward. Pray for guidance and believe in yourself.

Chapter Four: Forgiveness Is Life Fuel

"Look at 9/11 – there is an opportunity to forgive or to hate some more – which do you want to live with?"
~ Migdoel Miranda

In 1993 I left Puerto Rico and I arrived in the U.S. as a newly awarded scholarship recruit for a college baseball program in Tennessee. My college advisor asked me what I wanted to study. All I really knew then was that I wanted to help people move in their bodies better and that I could play baseball. Since my English was not so great, when I expressed, "I want to become a physical therapist, kinesiologist, and personal trainer," she heard, "I want to help disabled people walk better."

It took me until my junior year to realize that I was on track in the Special Education field and that she and I had not been on the same page at all. Despite that insight, and the two years that it took for me to realize it, I knew there was a bigger picture. So, I continued my education and graduated with a desire to help kids with special needs get to the Olympics. I felt that it was a noble goal both for them and me, but when I got more deeply involved in the field, I realized the biggest obstacle to achieving our goal of the Special Olympics, was their own parents' resistance. Somehow inside of me, I felt very clearly that this was not my battle to fight, and moreover, that it was a sign. So, I left that battle behind and got back on track with my dream of becoming a trainer.

Now, being a good student of life and the school of hard knocks, I was on my knees on the ground twice in my life with no money and all that goes along with that. I have shared with you a bit about the first time it happened in Florida and how I was able to recover thanks to thinking good thoughts, having a good attitude, and being fortunate enough to have good friends. Somehow, I survived. But the second time felt a whole lot harder because I was older and I had more responsibility than ever before. When I learned big life lesson number two, I had gotten married and was blessed with one beautiful bouncing baby boy.

As fate would have it, I evidently needed further personal growth, and Austin, Texas was the backdrop for that growth. It also proved to be the definitive turning point towards success in my career. Every challenge I faced in Austin was even harder than the ones that I faced the first time around in Florida, yet, I am grateful. This time I took note of how I did it so that I could share it with you now. This is the single most powerful message that literally saved a my inner life: forgiveness.

I had many opportunities to put this one into practice because I held anger from my childhood about a few key events. One of those events was when my childhood girlfriend told me that she did not believe that I was 'the one.' This was the first instance in my life where I was confronted with dishonesty, despair, distrust, and lack of integrity. In fact, that was the first time I felt pain from the outside penetrate into my physical being. It struck me and I felt the power of how my emotions could physically affect me. I did not understand that before that turning point in my life. I became intrigued by the pain in my chest and why this life event hurt me in that specific area of the body. Later, I came to learn that the zone of the Heart is the zone of love, where the body feels the dispro-portionate giving or receiving.

Another life event that brought me the clarity around the cycle of forgiveness was when I had to deal with smoking every time I arrived home to my parents' house where I grew up. Everyone around me smoked cigarettes, which conflicted with my desire to be physically 'clean' in order to play sports. My environment did not me take me seriously. I was carrying the burden of uncommunicated conversations that were eating my heart's desire to make more of my life. It was heavy and hurtful. I was full of sorrow and rage because everyone was making me breathe their second-hand smoke at home and in my culture. I kept my resentment bottled up inside which made me feel powerless. This was only interrupted when I realized that I needed to forgive myself for being angry about feeling powerless. I never told anyone else how their smoking negatively affected me.

Lastly, I was tested in forgiveness as a result of a religious leader who placed his private parts on me as a teenager. I was so young and so involved in the church that I thought it was a normal act of love. After someone whom I revered and trusted as an authority of God did this to me, I distrusted my faith and religion. These had always been sources of strength for me in the past. I resented that a man in a position of power, who was so "respected," had used me as his source of physical satisfaction. I was amazed that someone could be so selfish in the name of God, and it caused my world to crumble around me. I learned about a whole new level of deceit because this man used God, whom I loved, and whose authority I had always been strictly taught not to question, as a means of manipulating me. I was taught to unquestioningly do what I was told when it came to God and the church. I thought it would be disrespectful if I said no or protested in any way. It is nearly incomprehensible, even now, to think about the pressure I was under as a young child as a result of that one person's abuse of authority. I do thank God that I continued to learn throughout my life about the healing power of forgiveness and have been able to apply it efficiently to this situation. This took me on a journey towards profound forgiveness, since the measure of forgiveness had to be in proportion to the suffering inflicted.

I am so thankful now for having had these life experiences. Today I can say that I am grateful that these hard things are a part of the story of my life. Of course, these people did not attend to do right by me, but their mistakes have helped me to grow and find new freedom through forgiveness. Each of these people could never know how they changed my life and how they added incentive to my future success. So, believe me when I tell you that forgiveness really is life's fuel.

Most of my clients when they first come to me are focused merely on their physical fitness, health, and strength. They are focused solely on achieving desirable bodies. They celebrate when they achieve desirable goals such as weight loss, lower body fat, increased stamina, and vitality. But oftentimes, I am amazed at how people bring negative emotions to their training sessions. I have seen negative emotions such as anger, resentment, blame, and entitlement expressed at the same time that people are trying to get positive results through their training. I realize that they are not aware that they are leaving a trail of pain as they workout, instead of a trail of joy, because they are unwilling or unable to recognize their own role in creating their life outcomes. If they could only know that they are wanted, that they are loved, and that they are exactly where God wants them to be, then they might be the first ones to acknowledge and resolve the sources of pain in their own lives. Everything would change for them. If they could find forgiveness, they would experience a better life, and faster, measurable, physical results in the gym. I personally know this to be true. I understand that saying the words, 'I forgive you,' is a lot easier than the actual act of forgiveness, which requires you to hold your heart in your hands.

Forgiveness is seeing life with true clarity. Your life cannot be about judging others in their choices and actions, it can only be about taking responsibility for your interpretation of what others are choosing to do, and what you are choosing to do in your own life. When you do not forgive someone, it is like stabbing yourself in the leg and expecting someone else to hurt. This concept unfortunately takes a while for each of us to fully accept.

There is an old Cherokee legend that tells of a story between a wise elder and his grandson. The elder is educating his grandson about the internal battle people face. He said, "My son, the battle is between two wolves inside us all. One is evil. The other is good. The evil wolf is anger, envy, jealousy, sorrow, regret, greed, arrogance, self-pity, guilt, resentment, inferiority, lies, false pride, superiority and ego. The good wolf is joy, peace, love, hope, serenity, humility, kindness, benevolence, empathy, generosity, truth, compassion and faith." The grandson thought about it for a minute and then asked: "Which wolf wins?" The old Cherokee simply replied, "The one you feed." And this legend is still true today with people. Which of your wolves will you feed?

> *"Forgive them as they have no clue what they are doing."*
> ~ **Jesus Christ (paraphrased)**

Forgiveness is an irrational act. How do you forgive somebody who has hurt you? Regardless of how your forgive someone, it is essential that you do it for the quality of your own life. When you forgive, you release the burden of the hurt and make room for new light in the form of new relationships, new opportunities, and wiser decision making in your life. Holding on to the pain from the past does not give you fuel to move forward in the present. This is not about letting the other person 'off the hook,' or about whether they were right or wrong, or if you agree with them or not. It just means you want to lighten your own load so that your own life is better. It means that you are willing to move past a painful situation so you can get on with what's next for you.

Being thankful for the opportunity to forgive is just as important, actually, as it reminds the universe that you are ready to move on with your life. And it is also a path to healing for your physical body because the stress and anger that come from not forgiving someone can damage all your systems.

The point of interior fitness is to develop greater resilience to handle life's challenges because they will always be there! It is not what happens, but how you handle it that determines the quality of your life. If you go one step further to have gratitude for life's challenges, you will always find joy in your life, and never feel like a victim of circumstance.

Once you have committed to actively practicing forgiveness, you will have learned the lesson of the situation at hand that God is teaching you. Just be sure to continue practicing forgiveness in your daily decision-making going forward. Be sure to let go of any pain, anger, or resentment that took root in your heart in order to truly forgive. Sometimes people hold onto pain, resentment, self-righteousness, fury, etc., so tightly that their bodies get stuck in the suffering, and this suffering becomes their normal discomfort zone, and is then reflected in various physical dysfunctions and symptoms. For example, I use a technique through my work to help people 'unfreeze' their diaphragm so they can breathe again. It is an amazing experience for them when they breathe for the first time! The body is happy as it can inhale more oxygen and feel more life within.

Just as important as forgiving other people, is forgiving yourself. This is usually even harder than forgiving other people. Forgive yourself for:

- Not having clarity in making decisions.
- Not taking responsibility for your life choices.
- Using other people to create outcomes that hurt either you or others.

- Directing negative emotions like anger, jealousy, rage, or hatred at others to hurt them.
- Participating in situations that went against your inner authority or better judgment.
- Trying to manipulate or control others, even if you felt it was out of love.
- Gossiping about other people.
- Not respecting yourself enough.
- Not trusting yourself and your abilities.
- Feeling imperfect.
- Not loving yourself as you are.

Once you find these things in yourself, you should forgive yourself. Ignoring this invitation will actually cause you greater conflict. If and when you forgive yourself, then your life will change, because what you think about is what you create in your life. It will empower you.

The reason why I moved my family from Miami to Austin was because one of my clients had insisted that I come and work for him there. I gave great consideration to his offer, and we took a leap of faith and moved. Shortly after our arrival there, I learned that he was getting a divorce, and the business that he invited me to come work in, was family-owned and subsequently destroyed by the divorce. I gave up a comfortable life in Miami with steady income from clients for nothing on the other end in Austin! I had used my all my resources. I had trusted this guy enough to move my family across the United States, and now what? For what?

But after arriving in Austin, I discovered the power of forgiveness. I realized that God used this 'friend' to bring me to the next level. The purpose of that 'friend' in my life was not for me to work for him, but for me to move to Austin. I realize now that I needed the stability that Austin provided in order for me to go back and handle all the hurt that was lurking inside of me from my past. I began to address my past pains only once I got there.

My mentor, Paul Chek, teaches that we need to love people without necessarily liking them. It was in that moment that I had to choose whether I should eliminate this guy from my life or should I learn the lesson of forgiveness in a deep and profound way by loving him? So, in my particular situation, I essentially had to choose between being wounded for life or rising above the seeming reason that I moved to Austin in order to meet the as yet-unseen opportunities afforded to me there. I chose to forgive.

This was when I reached into the doors of my heart to learn what I really had to give to another person, when I felt like I had the least to give. I discovered the power of forgiveness by gathering my thoughts and recognizing my innate intelligence as the proverbial 'acres of diamonds' inside of me. I welcomed the fire to begin to polish me. I concentrated not on my old strategy of saving my money (which had been my primary financial strategy up until then), but on my new strategy of making more money, because I realized that making more money would move me farther forward. In addition, I truly forgave that then divorced client who lured me to Austin with broken promises, for what felt like the biggest betrayal of my life. Only when I truly forgave him did my life and my business turn around. And it happened almost instantaneously! I let go and life got better. God was providing for me and my family as I remained obedient to His call to go to Austin.

I was under so much stress in trying to make a new life in Austin that I began to search for something to anchor my spirit. I felt lost in a new city with my family. I certainly did not seek out a church to anchor it after what had happened to me. So, I decided to take a mental journey back to my childhood in order to try to understand it with new eyes. I chose to do something that would allow me to connect with myself more deeply. I forced myself to revisit my childhood and think like the kid I was then. I did not know at the time that merely thinking back to my childhood would help me to balance my daily life, but it did. I came to realize that what I was looking for was to play again. I wanted to do activities purely for the love of them. I wanted to rediscover clear and unadulterated passion in my life only for the simple emotional income. The desire to get to know myself again as a kid, to reconnect with my childlike world, was assisted greatly by the awesome collection of pictures that my mom had saved and was kind enough to mail to me. I noticed that when I wore shirts of the same colors as I did in my childhood, that I felt an even greater connection to my former self. Healing happened as the kid in me and the adult in me reconnected. It was awe-inspiring to follow my train of thought as a child through those pictures.

I bought a bicycle so that I could remember the freedom that I felt riding through my neighborhood and jumping around as a boy. I did things for the joy of playing. I needed to erase the image of my bicycling in Miami out of necessity, and replace it with the joy of playing. Even today, I still ride that bicycle and jump around, and I have even added driving remote control cars to my current toy box in an effort to further fuel my childlike passion.

Even though I have coached many people through this process, it might not work for everyone. However, it is certainly worth trying, even if you do not have fond childhood memories. Even if your childhood was not ideal, know that you were chosen to experience the nastiness so that today, you would be a stronger adult with a much broader view of life. Your will and your backbone are stronger so that you can hold your head up high and shine like a beacon of light for others who might be walking behind you on that same path.

The key to success is not found in accumulating knowledge and showing off. Instead, it comes from the ability to forgive our master teachers. I learned to love myself again, and in gratitude, I held my flag high and began to rebuild my life. My mind, my being, and my presence all became stronger. I actively and outwardly respected myself more. I honored my temple and learned to live a life filled with gratitude. Forgiveness helped to propel me forward with new momentum. Let forgiveness be your life fuel too!

Take a Moment For Your Interior Fitness:
- Hug someone, and then let them hug you back.
- Cook, then feed yourself with quality nutrition that you will actually enjoy.
- Forgive someone else's trespasses.
- Then forgive yourself for your own.
- Assess the quality of all of your relationships.
- Resolve or dissolve the problematic relationships in your life.
- Forgive yourself for entering the problematic relationship in the first place.

Forgiveness is Life Fuel- This is the key to success. When you recognize & eliminate anything that is holding you back, you will move forward. If you want a successful business, relationship, or career that is genuinely happy, then forgiveness is necessary to accomplish your goal. The life fuel of forgiveness is what heals the interior in order for the exterior to improve.

Chapter Five: Live Whole-Heartedly

"Few are those who see with their own eyes and
feel with their own hearts." ~ Albert Einstein

Have you heard the common saying: *'Follow Your Heart'*? This is not simply an old wives' tale. It is truly a key to your fitness success.

The heart is not just a body organ, but also a special place that is full of life. It is the one place that you literally cannot live without knowing truth. The beliefs that live in your heart have the power to take you exactly where you need to be at any given moment in order for you to live to your highest purpose. Your heart conspires with your dreams to achieve happiness. Your emotional happiness is your heart's true function. Its very nature is designed to give you life force energy, which circulates desire and love throughout your body. It guides you without interruption or guessing games, if you only listen to it.

Your body is made from the blueprint of God. You have only to feel your heart in order to understand this to be true. Your heart paces out the measure of your life, beat by beat, without your needing to think about it. Stop searching for answers outside you and go within. When you do, you will find the metaphysical and intuitive clarity you need. In the words of Carolyn Myss, "Your biography becomes your biology," and over time, you will begin to see physical confirmation of your own perfection. Correspondingly, if your body is experiencing any symptoms, there is a very real reason for them. Try to interpret where they came from in your emotional journey.

Your heart needs to be in shape since it is a muscle like any other muscle of your body. When your heart is in shape, you can think more clearly and be full of vitality without the need to stimulate your hormones with drugs. Coffee, sugar, and drugs serve only to corrupt, distort, or even numb your natural heart rhythms. You cannot make any decisions in alignment with your heart's desires, because its rhythm is interrupted, and therefore, it no longer speaks clearly to you. The focus of this book is on your interior fitness including nourishing your mind, living your core values, and becoming conscious of your perceptions of the world around you.

Your life is happening now, not yesterday, not tomorrow, but today. Now is your only opportunity to live your real life. If you are unsatisfied with your status, then propel yourself on to your best. It is time to be different on purpose, to live whole-heartedly. You cannot do that if you are in self-protection mode.

If you feel defensive in any way, your heart will put up invisible shields to protect you. Your heart is the emotional processing center of your body and your life. When you feel vulnerable, it can be a blessing or a curse. If a negative emotional experience hurts you it will shake you to your core. If you are rewarded for that vulnerability, with a positive emotional experience, it will also shake you to your core. Either way, when you show up whole-heartedly, without holding a piece of yourself back from life, you will be shaken to your core with the depth of the emotions you experience.

When you live whole-heartedly, you cannot sell out to fear, material possessions, self- image, money, or other people's opinions. Your spirit transcends your body in the form of ambition, dreams, and desires. When your heart is ready to drive you to the next level spiritually because of these ambitions, dreams, and desires, it will no longer settle for living small. Your heart will be fueled by these spiritual components to drive your body and life. You will no longer be satisfied to trade your precious life force energy and just go through the motions, make mediocre decisions, or play it safe to 'just get by,' because your heart will not allow it.

Living in your comfort zone means that you are not taking the necessary risks to reach your true desires. Living whole-heartedly means answering the call to move forward from this comfort zone and to be all you are meant to be in this lifetime. It also means that your life will be bigger than it has ever been and you will be singing your soul song to the world. You will make better choices. You will give life to your dreams and you will let your talents shine. You will take more risks to follow your dreams. You will cultivate your power, and therefore your level of fitness, by following your whole-hearted desires.

If you do not commit yourself to living whole-heartedly, you are actually asking the core of your being to sleep through your life. If you do not commit to positive action then, by definition, you are giving your energy to inaction and being stagnant. If you are not inspired to live whole-heartedly, you are dimming your inner light and living according to what other people define as your potential. This "brakes on" way of living gives away your power by allowing external forces to diminish your life.

A very common example of this dynamic is found in people who seem to believe that they are superior to everyone else because of their religious status, financial condition, or educational level, for instance. They perceive themselves at a higher level compared to the rest of the world because they are on a journey to 'sainthood,' financial security, or supreme knowledge. However, these people tend to not engage in true relationships with other human beings, except those that they perceive to be on their same level. Towards the rest of world, they behave holier than thou, snobby, arrogant, and in demeaning ways as a defense mechanism to exploring their own deficits. Until they drop these separatist mechanisms, they will not be in harmony with their true heart, and therefore not progress in their inner fitness.

Moreover, if they choose to be condescending, arrogant, or elitist, they are preaching from their darkness, or confusion within them- selves. They are limiting their hearts, shrinking their minds, and constricting their experience. Ironically, we are all naked here and we are just trying to fool each other when we play these games. We are already exposed and no degree of posturing behavior can create enough cover for inauthentic presence. We cannot hide.

 Each person has his own idea of what the true meaning of his life is. People write their own personal history in their minds according to their worldviews of the reasons for our human existence here on Earth together. Each person has the ability to see clearly and, many times, people deliberately choose the path of confusion in order to avoid what the heart sees as truth. The mind is overriding the heart! You can see this in dysfunctional, toxic relationships where the one individual knows they need to get out and away to stop the abuse, yet he or she chooses to stay with a partner any- way, ignoring the heart's message of the truth.

Your job in that situation is to love them without liking them so your own life experience is whole-hearted. And if you recognize this attitude of superiority and elitism in yourself, and feel that you are avoiding life experiences because of it, then you have work to do on your interior fitness. Each person is special in his own ways.

That being said, living whole-heartedly is not necessarily always a smooth experience. It will mean breaking old habits and limitations that you have placed on your life and requires that you be honest about your relationships. It means expanding your inner truth by having honest conversations with yourself about what is living in your inner shadows. You have treasure buried in your blind spots. By living whole-heartedly, you break your internal emotional barriers.

Living whole-heartedly is about choices. Choice is the most powerful force on the planet because it needs to precede everything that you do in your life. It even comes before love, because you have to choose to love. It even comes before forgiveness because you have to choose to forgive. You have the privilege to choose how you want to show up in this life. Showing up in a good state of mind will help you make better choices to assist you in your quest for interior fitness.

Life is complicated by virtue of nature's dynamic growth. Just watch a hurricane, a volcanic eruption, or an earthquake and you will observe multiple things happening at the same time. To take it all in at once is just not possible. You have to choose what you want to pay attention to in each given moment, then the overall chaos inside you will cease, bit by bit.

While there are so many things happening in the world simultaneously, you are living your little life on this Earth. Your body is generating cells, you are breathing, and blood is circulating throughout your interior, all passively happening while you are actively choosing how to live your life. And make no mistake, you must choose how you are living your life because it becomes whatever you make it.

You can hide or protect or turn off part of your heart to save it for something only you can know, or you can make the choice to live whole-heartedly and fully participate emotionally in every experience life has to offer you. The choices you make are not going to always feel good. Life comes only through endings, and endings do not always feel good. Ironically, not making a choice is a choice in and of itself, so your life will live on with or without you in some way.

Here are some of the choices you have to confront on the path to interior fitness:

- Your level of survival: do you want to struggle, labor through life, and barely make it or do you want to feel strong, powerful, and resilient?
- Your fears: is anything bigger than you in your life? If yes, are you ok with that?
- Your achievements: where do you want to win more?
- Your tranquility: how do you honor and relate to your inner self and higher power?
- Your clarity: how do you choose to receive and interpret your insights, to know yourself, and to integrate your curiosities into your life?
- Your healing: how much do you want to let love be a guiding force for you and others?
- Your nature: in what ways do you choose to be connected to the natural world?
- Your balance: where is your balance point between being and doing, working and taking time off, being independent and recognizing there is a greater context for your life?

As you make your choices, own them. Interior fitness means no more creating stories to make yourself right and then starting fights with others just because they do not think like you. Instead, go beyond your physical world senses to use your inner knowledge about living whole-heartedly to make different choices. Let your energy and decision-making come from your whole heart instead of having decisions made for you passively. You cannot live your whole-hearted life while sitting on the sidelines.

Take a Moment For Your Interior Fitness:
Here are some of the best tips that you can use to enhance your interior *and* exterior fitness:

- Go see how many push-ups you can do right now, and then add one more when you do them tomorrow.
- For every push-up, pair it with an air squat (body weight squats).
- Do not tell anyone how many push-ups you did until you are really happy about the outcome and cannot wait to celebrate your accomplishment.
- Look in the mirror and say, "I am going to love you better today than I did yesterday."
- Learn to feel your heart as your personal gauge for the degree to which you are living whole-heartedly. There are teachers who specialize in helping you understand and feel your heart, such as www.heartmath.org.

Live Whole-Heartedly- Following your heart is the key to enjoying tranquility and peace. This will ultimately take you to the magical place where you were meant to be. That does not mean that there will not be struggles along the pathway. Just do not allow the struggles to define you. Keep on your path to your destiny. You will always win by following your heart.

Chapter Six: Be Open to Be Fit

"The only way that we can live is if we grow. The only way that we can grow is if we change. The only way that we can change is if we learn. The only way we can learn is if we are exposed. And the only way that we can become exposed is if we throw ourselves out into the open. Do it. Throw yourself."
~ C. Joy Bell

If you have your hands closed in a fist, you cannot receive abundance. If you have your arms folded across your chest, you cannot receive a hug. When you know everything already, you cannot learn. When you are closed, nothing new can come into your world. In other words, you can either build your fort, or you can defend it. If you are busy defending, you are not building. This means you get stuck where you are physically and mentally because you must receive new input in order to change your results. As Einstein said, "The same mind that created a problem cannot solve it." You must be open to new ideas, habits, and practices in order to actually change your life.

Hopefully, you saw the video of my presentation at the CHEK conference in San Diego. If you have not seen this video yet, then check it out on my website www.diofitness.com and click the 'About' tab. While I was speaking to the audience, I was not aware of my words or my body language. I was just present in the moment with the audience. I was confident, secure in myself, and speaking to my mentors in the audience. I can repeat the essence of what I said because it is my true story, but somehow, I have forgotten what actual words I used because I spoke from my heart in the moment.

The language of the heart is the only one that matters. I arrived in Jackson, Tennessee for college with less than a tourist's understanding of English, except for baseball words, which I knew from TV. Since I attended college on a baseball scholarship, I was assigned a private tutor and took English as a second language so that I could improve my communication skills. I was very quiet for the first two years and just absorbed everything. An older baseball player from Memphis took me under his wing, showed me kindness, and helped me informally with my homework. He took the time to ensure that I understood what was being asked of me so that I could respond appropriately. Then, in my junior year, I began feeling more comfortable in English, my confidence increased, and my life began to get better, even if I still had a strong foreign accent! Eventually, I realized that it was a great accomplishment of mine to not only go to college, but to graduate from college, in a second language. I learned that repressing my thoughts because of my lack of English skills was not good for my own physiology and could even cause disease. I needed to express myself. And so I did, even though I made lots of mistakes and even though I had a strong accent, God made sure that there were kind people in the South to balance out those who made fun of me. And, I never realized how much I had overcome until I began to rewrite and deeply edit this book with a language and cultural specialist.

There are two primary reasons why I have shared this personal story about my path to full personal expression with you: authenticity and the importance of truth. Authenticity means telling the truth to yourself as well as expressing the truth to others. I no longer repress my feelings, and my body thanks me for that. The same is true for you. If you are lying to yourself, even if you are just stretching the truth even a little bit, then you are putting unnecessary stress on your body and therefore holding yourself back from advancement. Lies cause misunderstandings and unnecessary drama of which take a toll on your interior fitness and your relationships with other people.
Lying causes people to not trust you because they often see

through your lies and distrust you well before you are able or willing to admit that you lied to yourself and them. Instead, you persist, and try to convince yourself of your own lie instead of focusing on maintaining the trust with the other person first and focusing on telling the truth to both him or her and yourself. The important issue from that moment on is no longer the lie itself, but the fact that you have lost your authenticity and the trust that you used to have with that person.

My aunt once told me, "People never change despite their proclaiming loudly that they have changed to anyone who will listen." When people lie, they suppress themselves to try to please others, but their heart speaks so loudly through their actions that it reveals them. Unfortunately, this causes them to live a dark, cloudy life trapped in their own lies and never to move forward. Worse yet, is when the liar perpetuates the lie, and even tells different versions of it to the same audience, making things worse by further reducing his credibility. You can avoid all this by simply being authentic to yourself and others.

When you are authentic in your life and genuinely speak the truth from your heart, you can be confident that you found the right words in the moment. Trust yourself and this process and then let go of outcomes which were never in your control in the first place.

The intensity of the sun reminds us of the strength and power of God. There is no need to look straight into the sun; instead, its presence can be felt simply by its rays of light and heat. The fact that the sun illuminates many places at the same time allows many people to experience its light, heat, energy, and therefore, God's presence, at the very same time as you.

Transparency is another high value of mine, similar to authenticity, because what you see is what you get. You will never have to guess where you stand with me because I will tell you. And I expect you to respect me enough to do the same. There are no judgments, projections about who you are, or assumptions about you or anything else because I really want to know you. And I really want you to know me. Life is too short to play games and transparency is the fastest way to get clarity in relationships.

"Be kind, for everyone you meet is fighting a hard battle."
~ Plato

Respect the people you come in contact with because everyone is doing their best to live through life. Their best might not meet your expectations, but they are doing the best they can with what they know. The energy that you send out is what you get back. Respecting others is respecting yourself.

One example of the need to be respectful is not blaming your parents for who you turned out to be, because you are in charge of your life now, not them. They did what they thought was best for you with what they knew at the time and the resources they had at hand. After the age of somewhere between 18 and 21 in most societies, you are considered an adult and on your own. It is no longer appropriate for you to blame anyone else for your bad behaviors. Your life is yours to respect and take responsibility for in every way.

I have respected people under seemingly unusual circumstances in the past, and I would like to share some of those stories with you so you can see that when you relate to others with respect, it can support your own interior fitness in a positive way.

The first story is about religion, which can trigger all kinds of emotions for many people. I was raised as a Catholic in Puerto Rico. I have had many conversations about religion with friends, family, church-going neighbors, and members of my congregation, but the best conversation about religion occurred when I spoke with an atheist. Despite the difference in our views, we had a lively and dynamic exchange about our perspectives. We both respected our views and there was no need to fight in defense of either side. As a matter of fact, we hugged after the conversation was over. I challenge you to love those that think differently than you as an exercise in flexibility. When you do, you will see how your body begins to change as it follows your mind's lead to be flexible.

"People take different roads seeking fulfillment; just because they're not on your road does not mean that they've gotten lost."
~ The Dalai Lama

Here is another story of what I consider the ultimate respect. My client, Bobby, was a 67 year-old man who did not believe he could stand on a balance board. In my mind, I believe that perhaps someone close to him said he would never be able to balance well on it. So maybe, he himself then never believed that he could and allowed that comment to own him.

One day, I placed him on the balance board without initially telling him what it was. I began speaking with him about daily things to distract him, while he successfully was balancing on the balance board. After less than a minute, I announced to him that he was actually already standing on a balance board. It was that easy! He looked almost embarrassed as the prejudice of limitations instilled by someone else was erased from his mind. He was surprised, in awe, and happy! He did not even know what a balance board looked like until I told him he was standing on one. Instead, he had blindly believed the comment and limited his own abilities in his own mind without even knowing what a balance board was based merely on what someone else had said to him in the past.

Sadly, people limit themselves all too often in their own minds based on others' comments in similar ways. But I respected Bobby enough to tell him the truth and believed in him, so that he could overcome that mental limitation and believe in himself as well. This experience could have been one of those that actually physically could possibly cause cancer wherein you allow someone else to plant a negative thought in your mind and you accept it as truth. Fortunately, merely by performing the physical act of unknowingly getting on the balance board successfully, Bobby was able to overcome those odds. You can learn more about this concept by watching www.thecureismovie.com. I am not a 'magic' trainer. I just believe that my clients can do things with their bodies that they cannot even imagine that they can do. If I do not believe, I cannot be helpful to clients who need positive reinforcement to go beyond their own limitations. People do not get into poor physical condition overnight, nor is their physical condition only physical. That is what interior fitness is all about and the reason for this book.

Some of the most basic limitations that are placed in my clients' minds, and therefore their bodies, are placed there by doctors. While I recognize the importance of surgeons defining physical limitations post-surgery for the average Joe so that he does not in any way jeopardize the positive outcome of his surgical procedure during the healing phase, I particularly love to design alternative ways of achieving the same results but with different mechanics. For instance, if a surgeon tells my client not to squat, then how does my client use the toilet? The reality is, my client does have bathroom needs to meet and if he is not bedridden, he will need an alternative way to get into the seated position; otherwise, as a practical matter, he will ignore the doctor's order and simply squat. My specialty is in modifying the basic squat, or any physical movement, to achieve the same outcome, but in a different way that will not be physically detrimental to the client. So, in this example, I might reduce the tempo of the squat, provide an assistive device to reduce the load on the site such as a stick, and have a family member help hold them to reduce the load as well. The bottom line is, people need to use the bathroom, so they are going to squat one way or another, and I prefer that they be taught the less damaging way to further reduce the possibility of post-surgical injury, instead of simply telling them 'do not squat.'

Another medical issue that bothers me is when a practitioner says with so much certainty that a patient only has X number of days left to live. I find this completely inappropriate because no one but God knows how many days a person will live. In addition, putting this grave 'news' in the mind of a human being can be extremely psychologically damaging. Words such as, 'there is only so much time left', or 'you should not expect a full recovery,' or 'you cannot lift more than X lbs,' can easily translate into psychological limitations that have strong physical manifestations for those patients. Therefore, I try never to do that. I do, however, believe in setting reasonable goals and constantly assessing and reassessing to meet the clients' needs.

Most people find it very difficult to disagree with authority figures; therefore, it is a rare person who can use that sense of disagreement with the limitation placed on him as fuel to prove the limitation wrong. If someone does place limitations on you that you do not believe in, then you must rise above that limitation. Just because someone else tells you that you have a limitation, does not necessarily mean that they are speaking a truth about you. Be open to your own possibilities, and if your desire is to overcome, then get advice from experts in health who are willing to take you to the next level. Doctors in the Western model are trained to be experts in disease, not health. As many have said before, the primary tools for recovery are cutting, poisoning and burning. If you want health, seek out a professional who specializes in health, such as a CHEK practitioner or other professional, and ask him/her to put together a wellness plan for you, not a disease plan.

Here is another story about one of my clients, 'Jack,' who had lived for twenty years without feeling his foot. His niece was a regular client of mine and mentioned to me that he could not walk. The Veteran's Administration doctors had told him that he would never walk again, and therefore he was in a wheelchair. I assessed him and I believed I could help him, mostly because he was very angry. He had lost his independence and was stuck in a wheelchair and his 'authority' figures had told him that he would never be any better. I believed that at least I could assist him to strengthen his upper body and to maintain some mobility while seated in his wheelchair. This would help him to regain a minimal level of independence.

But then, Jack told me that he still dreamed of walking again and even rowing out on the lake that was in front of his home like he used to. I was inspired by his angry spirit and hoped that he could channel this negativity into meeting these goals, as I knew that this was a client who did not want to settle for anything less. At that time in my career, I had no clue about the spine or nerves but I did know enough to believe in someone, and the possibility of being better and walking during his lifetime. The only thing I did intentionally was to stretch him, believe in him, and believe in his goals. Stretching in strategic and systematic ways helped him alleviate functional constriction and to increase circulation in his body. I also recall joking a lot with him, and smiling at someone who seemed to have never laughed and smiled like that before in his life.

At one point, I even put him in a rowboat and rowed him around on the lake for a session. I wanted him to experience that happiness again. Jack sat on the bench in the boat, and because he was a man of few words, he just took in the air and nature around him. I began to feel his trust in me increase at this point, and our working relationship became more synergistic as Jack was a person who needed to see results in order to believe in them. While it took some time to break the pattern of negativity that Jack had relied upon before, Jack finally figured out how to flip the switch and channel his anger into hard work with me to meet his goals of rowing and walking again.

We did twenty sessions, which was a significant investment of time and energy for both of us, and by the end of those sessions, Jack felt his foot again! He was feeling sensation in his foot where he had not felt anything in twenty years! Not only was he feeling his foot, he was walking with a walker again! It was a joy for him! While I never saw him row in the boat, he did improve, and was amicably discharged with permanent improvement in meeting his goal of walking, albeit with a walker for ambulatory assistance and stability.

For me, this experience was unique because I could see my intentions and hard work translate into improvement in Jack's physical body and actually transform it in a positive way. Jack not only was more physically fit, but internally fit as well. Then, I knew that I had reached my two goals with that client. Jack's interior fitness overcame the seemingly permanent, physical challenges. Interior fitness is powerful medicine. It is truly *health* care, not illness care!

Living your life with full vitality takes courage. Your experiences test your ability to be resilient and take action in the face of sometimes daunting odds. In order to do this, sometimes you will have to take a deep breath and push yourself beyond your comfort zone. This way, you can get more of what you want out of life.

Sometimes this means that you have to take action despite the fact that you do not feel ready yet to follow through on something, or do not know how to do it, or do not feel like you have the resources yet to do it. This is precisely when you need to take a leap of faith, make a decision from your whole heart, and allow yourself to trust in God and move forward anyway. The good news is that these moments in life are exactly when you should be most open to receive new courage, new knowledge, and new resources that will bless you to move forward.

Having positive motivators in place that are stronger than your natural resistance to change will help you leap over barriers that could otherwise hold you back. On your journey to interior fitness, thoughtfully define your motivation to reach your goals; otherwise it will be easy to slow down, or even stop midstream. Empower yourself with daily positive thinking and affirmations to help you achieve your goals, whatever they may be.

"The greatest gift you can give somebody is your own personal development. I used to say, "If you will take care of me, I will take care of you." Now I say "I will take care of me for you, if you will take care of you for me."
~ Jim Rohn

The last thing I have to say about being open to be fit is to be willing to accept that the resources and wisdom you need may come in unexpected ways. For example, you might want to get more exercise, but do not have the time to do it. Then one day when you arrive at work, you discover that the parking garage is under renovation, and you are forced to walk five extra blocks every day. At first, you may see this as a curse, but if you think positively, it may actually be the answer to your desire to get more exercise. You see, you will attract what you need. You attract the renovation to fulfill your desire for more exercise. You must be creative sometimes to perceive just how your desires and prayers are being answered. At first you may not appreciate the answer, as it may not be the exact answer you wanted, but do your best to stay open and receive it.

Take a Moment For Your Interior Fitness:
- Breathe deeply three times through your nose at least every hour today.
- Do not buy any special exercise equipment or clothing at first, just bring yourself.
- Take an 'e-tox' – turn off the TV, computer, and phone for at least half the day.
- Go for a walk at your own pace and enjoy nature.
- If you find yourself challenged and emotionally closed, remove yourself from the situation for at least eleven minutes, then come back to it and see how you feel then.
- Set yourself up to win by putting some structure around your fitness goals by breaking them into bite-size pieces. Schedule them so that you will actually do them like you would any other appointment or project.
- If you find it difficult to stay on track with your exercise plan, then take a personal survey of your relationships and environment to ensure that everything and everyone is really supporting you. You may need to do some external or internal housecleaning in order to improve your physical and interior fitness.
- Remember, any new habit, goal, routine, or relationship takes time and focus to grow. If you make fitness a priority and be patient but firm with yourself, you will achieve your goals.

- The most authentic part about interior fitness is the personal part that you do by defining your own motivations, desires, and needs, when no one else is watching.

Be Open to Be Fit- Please understand that in order to make changes in your life, you must break your routine and embrace new activities and ideas. Try to evaluate what exactly is holding you back from reaching your life goals. Could it be a result of your relationship with others? Your own dishonesty with yourself or others? Anger over past issues? Try to begin to measure your health and interior fitness by loving and caring more instead of looking at how much weight you have lost. Always make sure that the goals that you set are to please yourself and not anyone else, or they will be empty, unattainable goals.

Chapter Seven: Strengthen Your Abdominals

PIGLET: How do you spell love?
POOH: You do not spell it, you feel it.
~ Winnie the Pooh

While the fitness industry frequently emphasizes supplements, powerhouse training, fancy nutrition bars, and hard-core regimens, my philosophy is that optimal fitness is best achieved by living the basics every day. I recommend good sleep, quality nutrition, deep breathing, good positioning when exercising, good hydration with water, and avoiding negativity.

Once you get started with an exercise routine, fitness should start to feel good. There may be aches and pains along the way, but the progress you see in reaching your goals can be a great motivator for you to continue with your routine. How well you feel is a good indicator of how aligned you are with your interior fitness.

The difference between contemplating doing something vs. actually doing something is your interior fitness. That interior voice that motivates you to bear through current circumstances in order to achieve a positive outcome is your willpower at work. To help you stay basic in your fitness routine, feel your way to greater vibrancy, and walk the path of interior fitness. I am going to explore nutrition, passion, and business below in greater detail. These three things most commonly sabotage even the strongest sense of personal willpower.

NUTRITION

There are so many diets out on the market. People are constantly in search of the 'best' one. I have reviewed many diets, and the overall lesson that I have learned is that a true diet should consist of eating by what you feel and listening to your body. However, the enormous problem with this method is that people are so disconnected from themselves that they are no longer able to read their true nutritional needs by their cravings. Their cravings are hidden by a numbness that comes from eating packaged, boxed foods. These refined foods provide further insulation from their true feelings in the form of potbellies. That is the physical barrier to the emotional access. People also over-schedule themselves with projects, tasks, deadlines, and other people in ways that make nutrition not a priority in terms of the time that they allocate to it. This misallocation of time makes them further disconnected from the process of food preparation and consumption, as they often wait too long to even contemplate what or where they will eat. On top of this, they eat whatever they have chosen far too fast.

Ironically, it is exactly through the belly that you can discover your best nutrition, by monitoring the feeling as feedback you get in response to what you ingest. Those feelings become more difficult to assess, the greater the inflammation you have around your belly. Eating properly requires paying attention to your body and your emotions after you eat something. This is called Metabolic Typing® for customized nutrition. Metabolic Typing® simply means finding out how your body reacts to certain foods. By knowing your metabolic type®, you can control cravings, hunger, energy levels, emotions, and mental focus.

Metabolic Typing® identifies the system in your body that is effected by what exactly you just ate. Knowing this system, a list of foods that will help you come into balance can be recommended. If you feel tired, bloated, anxious, or irritable after you eat, then this methodology teaches you how to balance your proteins, carbohydrates and fats to help you feel better than you ever have before.

Below are some simple guidelines to use to determine whether or not you are eating properly for your metabolic type®:

- Note your appetite both before and after you eat.
- Note your cravings both before and after you eat.
- If the hunger and/or the craving is/are still there afterward, then what you ate is not of the proper metabolic type to satisfy you.
- Notice your mood, good or bad, both before and after you eat.
- Notice your ability to focus both before and after you eat.
- If you are still cranky or feel scattered after you eat, what you ate is not of the proper metabolic type® for you.
- Note your overall energy level: is it better or worse after you eat?
- Note if you are jittery both before and after you eat.
- If your energy is worse or your jitters are still there after you ate, your body is not getting the nutrition it needs.
- Note whether you feel bloated or gassy after you eat; if yes, your body is not digesting efficiently or you are simply not eating according to your needs.
- Note your heart rate after you eat. If it changes either up or down by five beats or more per minute, then you need to analyze what you are eating because your body is having a negative reaction to it.
- What you feel will change based on specific foods. These feelings can be felt for an hour or two both before and after you eat, so you have time to pay attention to what your body is telling you. There is no magic to it. Metabolic typing® is simply paying attention to what you eat and your body's reaction to it.

Food is what nurtures your body and all its parts, such as your brain, eyes, organs, muscles, and bones. Without proper nutrition, your systems will try to cover for each other to compensate for pain and weakness, however, over time, you will not only deplete the originally effected system, but the secondary system will be fatigued as well. Your physical systems need the proper fuel for your metabolic type®, so it is best to work with an advanced certified Metabolic Typing® advisor, who knows how to determine your metabolic type so that your body can get the most out of your nutrition. I am certified in Metabolic Typing® and would be happy to work with you to assess your personal needs.

Please go to the Metabolic Typing® section of my website: http://diofitness.com/metabolic-typing/ for more information on the process and pricing.

Metabolic Typing® encourages you to begin to pay attention to your own body's response to the foods that you choose to eat, in order to determine which ones are best for you. The potentially bad news for anyone who eats mindlessly without feeling is that you will have to begin a relationship with food in order to begin to feel the effects and messages your body is trying to tell you about the food you are eating. You can no longer eat on the run.
This methodology requires that you take the time to feel your body's responses to food. There are no shortcuts to create this new link between your nutrition and your body.

Many people predetermine which types of foods that they limit themselves to by their own strong ethical standards. These categories, such as carnivores, fruitarians, vegetarians, or those on special diets, which eliminate by definition entire categories of food, such as low carb diets, predetermine without any scientific basis what foods they are willing to eat. The Metabolic Typing® will be of limited use to these people, since they have already ruled out so many foods and are not willing to reintroduce them to their diet. For instance, vegetarians do not eat animal protein. That, however, does not exempt them from killing to eat. Like any other animal, humans need to kill to stay alive. Carrots, beans and seeds are living entities too, and vegetarians are killing them for their nutrition. So, the philosophical argument against killing life doesn't really stand up under scrutiny. We all have different needs for our nutrition, and while vegetarianism may work for some, for most people, it does not offer enough protein. In addition, many vegetarians have basic vitamin and nutrient deficiencies, as human beings are natural omnivores.

Whatever your specific nutrition philosophy, whether you are Fruitarian, Vegetarian, Pescetarian, carnivore or even a Breatharian, the key to feeling inner peace is in balancing the sugar level in your body. Sugar imbalances lead to feelings of rage, dizziness, headaches, spinal pain, nausea, impatience, and weakness. By controlling your sugar levels, you can stop this physiological pain and make yourself more level emotionally as well.

While there are guidelines about healthy nutrition that each one of us should establish for ourselves, the most important ones are to have good thoughts while you eat, to avoid watching TV while eating, and to avoid starving yourself. Eating is a natural part of life. You must eat to live! The most important part of eating together is to share and enjoy what you see on the table. After all, we should show gratitude for what has given its life for us to eat. We should eat in a peaceful, calm atmosphere in order to welcome food into our bodies and have good digestion. Enjoy the company that you keep at the table, allow your brain to rest, and your body to be satisfied. In the end, the choice about what you eat is up to you working with your body to determine your best nutrition.

PASSION

Humans are the only animals who can direct their passion con-sciously into creating an amazing life. A lot of people talk about living their passion, but how many people actually do it? Letting go of the familiar and comfortable status quo in order to pursue a life based on what feels good to your heart and spirit is still not the norm. Taking risks are encouraged but not if they are too risky. And when the people who love you want to protect you, they will encourage you to avoid risks.

These people are considered your tribe. They consist of your social groups such as friends, family, and colleagues. If you participate in behavior that does not conform to the norms of these groups, then, they will discourage it. Therefore, if you continue the per-ceived risky behavior despite their discouragement, then you risk jeopardizing your status in your tribe. If your behavior has a nega-tive outcome, then you might be abandoned or exiled by the group for your failure. If your risky behavior has a positive outcome, you still are not likely to be well received in your groups again because you have outgrown them. This growth is what produces success.

Living your life with passion is one of the fastest paths to success and interior fitness. You are certain to attract positive relationships that are in alignment with your goals, which can kick off new ad-ventures. It is exciting, fun, and rewarding. Passion encourages you to become resilient as a way to prepare your body to reach even bigger goals. The successful results of your passionate work will positively reinforce your path to healthy interior fitness.

How you make a living will ideally be driven by living your passion every day. If you are unhappy or chronically stressed by where you spend the majority of your waking hours, your body will reflect this negativity through ill health. It is really important that you take the necessary steps to live your passion, as it will bring joy, fulfillment, and a sense of personal meaning to your life. It seems as though living each day with passion should come naturally to us all, but unfortunately, many people keep doing the same thing every day sacrificing their passion to earn money, which negatively effects their health and fitness levels. At the same time, they keep expecting different results but not changing a thing except their gym or brand of running shoes! It boils down to doing what you love in life so that you are healthier, happier, and more fit. That is the path to interior fitness.

By working on yourself from within, you create space by throwing out those emotions and habits that no longer serve you. As you get to know yourself better, you will let go of the old, and make room for your new purpose in life, which is to help other people. As you understand the nature of your contribution, you naturally attract opportunities to do so. Creating your optimal life fitness starts from within and is driven by passion.

BUSINESS

As a businessperson, I am blessed to do what I love because I am living my passion. I have learned many lessons along the way that were not easy, but were always incredibly valuable. For example, many people think that doing good business is to try to duck difficult situations or people in the quietest possible way. Instead, I have found by years of my own experience that creating a win-win for both parties, while respecting their values, has become a better definition for me of a good business relationship.

I have done some deals that, in the eyes of hardcore business people, were deemed downright stupid, but resulted in good profits for me. I have done this by simply focusing on serving my clients to the best of my ability. I am extremely single-minded about customer service: I serve others as I want to be served and, as a result, things flow easily. When I approach situations with my inner desire to serve, it always ends up being good business with positive outcomes for everyone.

I grew up in a culture and an environment where loud voices and arguing were acceptable to get what you want or to simply meet your basic needs. After I came to the mainland U.S., I had to over-come that programming when in confrontational situations. It was difficult at first, but I learned that nobody felt satisfied when there was yelling involved, regardless of the outcome. As a result, now I never raise my voice and focus clearly on what I want and need in order to communicate it effectively. I have expanded my vocabu-lary, increased the repertoire of my possible responses, reduced my volume, and used appropriate language in my exchanges. These changes have proven to be invaluable strategies for crucial conversations. It helps to be nice, be honest, and produce a good product. Those things in addition to talent can lead to a profitable business. By working on my interior fitness, in addition to the exterior physical training that I had always done, I had combined emotional skills with physical skills to build what my accountant refers to as a profitable business.

When the economy got bad, it took a toll on my business, like many others. It seemed that people did not value their fitness as much as they did their money. People were punishing their bodies by working longer hours, driving farther to find a job, stressing over every day, things and thinking they were compensating for the downturn in the economy. Ironically, it is only through feeling good that people can create good things in their lives, including money. One critical way to make yourself feel good is to work out, but people did not make time to do it. So while my product was needed and had demand, many people suggested I get out of the training business because people would not spend their limited income on their fitness when they were feeling financially inse-cure. But I knew that what I do is actually the key for my clients to feel more vitality and resilience, which counter-balance negativity from a depressed economy. My clients benefit tremendously from increased energy, refocus on good nutrition, and leave my care rejuvenated and grateful. Their post-workout glow and revitalization is all that I need to see my own success. The emotional income that comes from helping my clients is extremely valuable to me.

Typically people put themselves last in their own lives, but while in session with me, they are the focal point of our time together. When we begin working together, I do not always know where the session will go because I listen to God and my client's specific needs in the moment in order to refine that day's particular program to best support their optimal wellness. I trust my own instinct and focus on their particular needs for their own wellness. By helping my clients to relax, train, and reset their bodies, their lives get better. It is impossible to beat up your body, and then expect it to be healthy in the long-term. The key to fitness is to train, not drain, your physical systems. I learned this early on from Paul Chek.

As I have grown greatly in my own interior fitness, I am now able to show my clients through my own example how spiritual and physical fitness can lead to life enhancement. So despite the bad economy, less discretionary income, and overall fitness being a diminishing priority, my business grew during the downtimes because people were attracted to my higher level of interior fitness. The double dose of interior and exterior fitness that I provided attracted more clients to my business. I found that people were looking for more than just a mere workout. From this experience, I realized that it was more important than ever for me to continue my own personal growth and walk my own talk. There was no other option as I needed new fuel to feed my own spiritual needs and to provide new energy for them each time they came into my presence. In the end, the supposed negative circumstances of an economic downturn turned out to be a positive blessing in my life as I rose to a higher level of interior fitness and it made me a better person and businessman. Because I accepted my own invitation to growth, despite the economic contraction, I continued working in my business, my dream and living my passion with clients.

The life lesson for each of my clients out of all of this was that especially in the downtimes, it is quintessential for them to focus on good nutrition, healthy lifestyle, and interior fitness. These three things, along with your workout program, will lead to improved exterior fitness. In this journey, try not to compare yourself to others, as it can discourage your efforts. Be aware of criticizing others because that is certainly where you are hardest on yourself. Give others the respect of trusting them to make their own choices, as their fitness needs may be different than yours. Let them choose. And lastly, be concerned about your own potential for self-sabotage in order to keep your interior fitness aligned.

Take a Moment For Your Interior Fitness:
- Get back to basics: feel your body before and after you eat to guide you to your best nutrition.
- Drink enough water daily and get quality sleep each night.
- Laugh!
- Make sure your fitness goals and routines are realistic. Set yourself up for success!
- Jump!!! This stirs up your lymphatic system to support detox. If you are in pain or cannot jump for some reason, then bounce while sitting on a Swiss ball or move all your limbs while sitting in a chair.
- Be nice to yourself, so you can be nice to others. You cannot give what you do not have, including positive support and love.

- Consider where your life needs more passion, and then take action to make it happen.
- Commit to that marathon or other long-term goal, but begin your training NOW!
- Know that you can achieve interior fitness with grace.

Strengthen Your Abdominals- Pay attention to how your body responds to different foods. Encourage habits that promote good digestion. Listen to what your body is telling you through its behavior, in particular, its reactions to different foods. Welcome the message and begin to change your food habits accordingly. None of us are perfect human beings, so respect yourself and others and the way we think.

Final Wisdom

Tell your heart that the fear of suffering is worse than the suffering itself. And no heart has ever suffered when it goes in search of its dream.
~ **Paulo Coelho**

Now that you know about the interior path to fitness, it is time to take action. When you do not feel ready to follow through on something, do not know how to do it perfectly yet, do not know that it will turn out the way you want to with any degree of certainty, and yet you still want to do it, you are at a pivotal point to move forward to new challenges in your life. You do not have to have everything perfectly aligned in order to rise up to the next step in your interior fitness. Do not procrastinate. There will never be a perfect time to move forward. Just take the resources that you have now, where you are now personally, and take a leap of faith in whatever it is that you want to achieve in your life.

Whatever the motivator, whenever it is stronger than the resistance to change, you will find yourself taking action and transcending obstacles, barriers and things that could keep you stuck somehow. There are times when this means trying something again when you have to scrape yourself up to do it, knowing that the first time did not go so well. Doing what you can in each moment with whatever you have to work with is an act of courage worthy of merit. Other people may not see it as such, but do not focus on the outside and others, focus on your path to interior fitness for a reason. This is your precious life and how you live your fitness is up to you.

You are the creator of your life experience. While it would be nice to pick and choose only the good parts you want, to really empower yourself to create what you want in your life, you have got to go through adversity. Not only do you need the nerve to get through a tough situation, you also need to know that you created it in some way to help you grow to a higher level.

So you have your love handles, the job that bores you, and a loved one that just does not seem to understand you. Trust that these situations are showing up to help you understand and address what does not work for you in order to create a better life. By owning your power in creating even the things that do not seem so wonderful, by seeing the bigger picture and by demonstrating the courage in the not-so-pretty parts of your life, you are empowering yourself to take the path to interior fitness. You are responsible for your life, your feelings and every result you get in your life. Nobody has more power in your world than you do to create your life. When you really get that, everything changes. The natural outcome of moving your mind is that you create your best life possible and reshape your body.

To make changes, look at your life right now. Look around you and see your life. Look in the mirror with an honest eye, but not a harsh one. Everything in your life is a manifestation of past choices, decisions, and commitments. Celebrate what you have, because it is what has gotten you to this moment. Being in gratitude literally helps you move to your next best level.

Now decide and write down what you want to do next to support your best level of fitness, in the next 90 days; then earnestly, deliberately, and consciously make the commitment to get it done. By the way, if you are working with a trainer that has not taken the time to assess your needs, you are flying blind. You do not have the baseline information you need to accomplish your goals on any level – physical, emotional or spiritual. Some testing needs to be done to bring clarity to your goals, such as: measuring your spinal curvatures, muscle range of motion, body fat and posture. Remember, the root of your pain, restrictions or excessive weight is the result of what is hiding deep within. Get a foundation in place so you have more to celebrate!

The path of interior fitness has certainly been helpful in my life and to those around me. For me, it has helped me grow as a friend, a husband, a dad, and a practitioner. I can soar, live, breath and feel as life was intended before my physical body came to touch the ground in this world. There is no absolute magical formula as to the best way for you to live your life. It is up to you to discover, nurture, and practice daily. This is the path of interior fitness. By moving your heart to a higher level of interior fitness, you can reshape your life *and* your body!

Appendix

<u>Adrenal Fatigue: The 21st Century Stress Syndrome</u> by James Wilson and Jonathan V. Wright
www.adrenalfatigue.org

<u>How to Eat, Move and be Healthy</u> by Paul Chek

Radical Forgiveness by Colin Tipping

Defy Gravity by Caroline Myss

www.Heartmath.org

http://www.thecureismovie.com/

Healthexcel Inc. - Metabolic Typing
http://www.healthexcel.com/

About The Author

Migdoel "Dio" Miranda

Inner Fitness Authority • Celebrity / Pro Athlete Trainer • Speaker

Austin, TX

dio@diofitness.com

A former pro baseball player who has been training and coaching speakers, amateur & professional athletes, models, celebrities and ordinary people since 2000, Dio Miranda B.S., CMT, teaches how to use simple daily strategies to live a life of exceptional health and vitality.

A native of Puerto Rico, Dio was recruited by Lambuth University in Jackson, Tennessee to play college baseball, and then went on to play baseball in the Independent League so he was quite familiar with the training necessary for high level athletes. While he was in college, Dio had the great experience of teaching disabled students as part of his degree program. He graduated college with dual degrees in physical education and special education. Dio found his ultimate dream somewhere between these two extreme levels of functioning as he was more and more intrigued by what could help the ordinary person achieve incredible health. Dio graduated from the Florida College of Natural Health as a certified massage therapist. Afterwards, he continued practicing as a trainer and massage therapist in the Miami area. Dio then further combined his interest in the spiritual and emotional aspects of the mind and body and how they affect physical performance and attended the prestigious CHEK Institute where he studied (C)orrective (H)olistic (E)xercise (K)inesiology. He has achieved the certifications of

69

Holistic and Lifestyle Coach II, Level III fitness trainer, and a high-performance exercise kinesiologist. In 2011, Dio was awarded international recognition as a CHEK Practitioner of the Year nominee.

While DioFitness is based in Austin, TX. Dio travels to work with clients internationally. His approach to fitness emphasizes healthier living both emotionally and physically in order to achieve greater vitality so that clients can live their lives to the fullest.

Dio is passionate about supporting young baseball athletes with age appropriate training, which is why he created his current DVD, *Play Ball Healthy*. www.playballhealthy.com

Dio is a dynamic public speaker who is very engaging, motivating and inspiring. He has spoken at many clubs, gyms, schools, and institutes. You can view one of his speeches online at www.diofitness.com.

When not working with his awesome local clients, or traveling to work with his celebrity clients, Dio's wife Nicole, son Kai, and daughter Kamila help him sharpen his own interior fitness.